Akathist
to
Saint George the Pilgrim

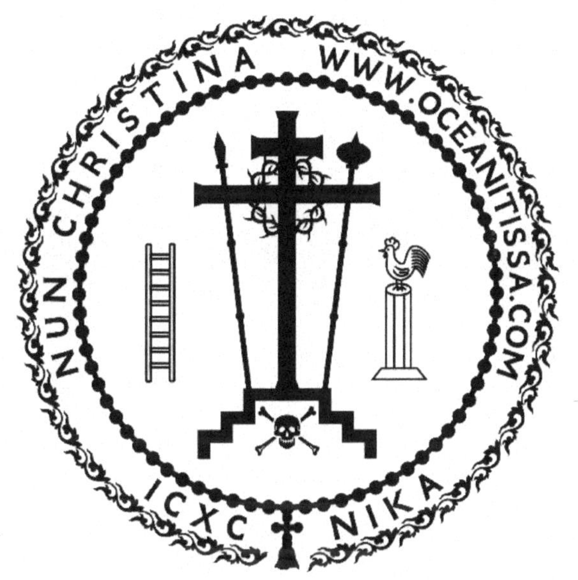

Anna Skoubourdis
Nun Christina

Published by: Virgin Mary of Australia and Oceania 2022 ©
oceanitissa@gmail.com
www.oceanitissa.com.au
Youtube: Nun Christina Oceanitissa

Subscribe to receive updates and Orthodox Christian creative media

www.oceanitissa.com

August 17

Akathist

Kontakion 1

All faithful, come to praise Saint George the Pilgrim who delighted the angels and called people to spiritual life through his wonderful life; for, zealously increasing the ardent gift of seeking and confessing God in travels, churches, and holy toils, he had become a source of joy and intercessor for those singing: Rejoice, Saint George, blessed pilgrim of Christ!

Ikos 1

Saint George, your heart was pierced from a young age by the call of the Savior, Whom you followed throughout your life; thus, barefooted, with your head uncovered, and carrying the Gospel of love in your hands, you became a sight to angels and men and arrived victorious in the heavenly Canaan, where you pray for those who sing to you:

Rejoice, pure youthfulness dedicated to God;
Rejoice, pinnacle of piety, which your blessed family marveled at;
Rejoice, pilgrim in the footsteps of the Savior in the Holy Land;
Rejoice, supplicant of humble spirit and broken heart;
Rejoice, you who lived all your life barefoot and with your head uncovered;
Rejoice, you who carried the Gospel among people incessantly;
Rejoice, ascetic who lived in the city as in the desert;
Rejoice, willingly poor who brings joy to the poor;
Rejoice, lover of the Psalter, which you learned by heart;
Rejoice, you who lived in prayer, vigil, and fasting;
Rejoice, you who knew the hour of your end, with prophetic eyes;
Rejoice, testimony and praise of public priesthood;
Rejoice, Saint George, blessed pilgrim of Christ!

Kontakion 2

Although you married through the Mystery of the wedding and were blessed by God with four children, you did not forget that the duties towards the family should not wither the zeal for the Lord's commandments. This is why, ardently going to church, giving alms, and praying incessantly, you also taught your sons to sing to the Holy Trinity: Alleluia!

Ikos 2

Fulfilling your duties as a father and husband, you lived spiritually, in prayers and fasting, therefore you heard in your heart the call of the Holy Spirit to a higher life, and, at the right time, you became a wanderer and a pilgrim, for which hear us:

Rejoice, you who from the dawn of life chose the good side;
Rejoice, youth, in which was ignited the longing for salvation;
Rejoice, son of wisdom, seeker of the kingdom of heaven;
Rejoice, pure sight, which shames the lust of the eyes;
Rejoice, faithful father, who showed your sons the way of salvation;
Rejoice, you who received the gift of prayer through your daughter;
Rejoice, ascetic mind, who has removed all indecency;
Rejoice, humble mind, who has overcome the pride of life;
Rejoice, the one in whom the Holy Spirit testified the mystery of adoption;
Rejoice, merchant who gave the ephemeral for the eternal;
Rejoice, you who rebuke those stifled by temporal things;
Rejoice, you who are rich in spiritual things;
Rejoice, Saint George, blessed pilgrim of Christ!

Kontakion 3

Saint George, when the right time arrived, you traveled to Jerusalem, where, after bowing before the Holy Places, you fasted for forty days, and a hermit prophesied that you would fulfill a high and arduous ministry, by which you will kindle piety in cold hearts; and, returning to your homeland, those who saw your deeds marveled and sang to Christ: Alleluia!

Ikos 3

Who will be able to tell the temptations you overcame during the fast in the Jordan desert? For, at the time of prayer, the devil sometimes troubled you with the temptation of vain glory, and at other times, he threw your shoes and hat, but you overcame him, promising God that all your life you will walk barefoot and with your head uncovered, for which we praise you, saying:

Rejoice, you who were overwhelmed with happiness when you reached the Holy Places;
Rejoice, the one flooded with the holiness of services and joy;
Rejoice, follower of Christ, through the forty-day fast;
Rejoice, good fighter, who defeated the dark snares;
Rejoice, you who were not afraid of the devil disguised as a plowman;
Rejoice, you who drove away the one who tempted you with pride;
Rejoice, humble thought, who despised his hidden cunning;
Rejoice, he through whom the delusion perished like smoke;
Rejoice, for in the church of the Resurrection, the candle in your hand lit up on its own;
Rejoice, you who walked all your life barefoot and with your head uncovered;
Rejoice, you who were crowned with the imperishable crown in heaven;
Rejoice, bird that longingly flew to the Promised Land;
Rejoice, Saint George, blessed pilgrim of Christ!

Kontakion 4

Moved by your ardent love for Jesus, you lived for a while among the Transylvanian believers, with whom you traveled many times to the Holy Places. Then, hearing about the numerous monasteries in Moldavia, you took shelter in the tower of Voivode Stephen at Piatra Neamț, from where, like a thirsty deer running to the springs of grace, you quenched your heart's longing and sang: Alleluia!

Ikos 4

For many years, you walked in the streets of the city of Piatra Neamț barefoot, with your head uncovered, carrying in your hands the Gospel and wandering staff and the whispers of unceasing prayer on your lips, which is how you, Saint George, became a preacher of the Cross, undefeated witness of holy teachings and intercessor for those who sing to you:

Rejoice, living Golgotha, who carried the holy Book among men;
Rejoice, you who were not ashamed of the Gospel of the Son of God;
Rejoice, letter written by the Holy Spirit, which the proud cannot understand;
Rejoice, living silence, who sees the futility of the words of the lawless;
Rejoice, humble herald, enlivened by heavenly power;
Rejoice, you who conquered the unseen enemies through humility;
Rejoice, pilgrim estranged from all fleeting care;
Rejoice, you who spoke only of the spiritual life;
Rejoice, suppliant in the Saint John church at night;
Rejoice, wise ascetic seeking dispassion;
Rejoice, life led according to the commandments of the Gospel;
Rejoice, you who made the body a slave and the soul king;
Rejoice, Saint George, blessed pilgrim of Christ!

Kontakion 5

Blessed one, loving the beauty of God's house, at night, you retired to the church of the village you reached. There, you raised prayers and did innumerable prostrations and the cunning enemy, seeing the zeal with which you called the name of Christ, once wanted to disturb you with his unclean appearance, but, burning him with the power of the Cross, you sang to God: Alleluia!

Ikos 5

Saint, prayer had become life and breath for you, for you talked to God all the time and in every place, and you were guided in this spiritual work by the Psalter of the Prophet David, which you loved from your youth and learned by heart so that you uttered it every day with a quick mind and feeling of heart, for which you hear from us:

Rejoice, icon of living Orthodoxy;
Rejoice, you who adorn the Church of Christ;
Rejoice, hidden torch between the walls of the holy places;
Rejoice, sorrowful intercessor for every creature in suffering;
Rejoice, you who, with much effort, performed the ascetic ordinances;
Rejoice, you who learned by heart the Psalms of David;
Rejoice, you who uttered it every day, walking through the streets of the city;
Rejoice, wise thinker of the Law of God;
Rejoice, you for whom the whole world has become a church;
Rejoice, you who learned to pray in spirit and in truth;
Rejoice, supplicant full of divine grace;
Rejoice, you who have been enriched by the knowledge of the priceless Pearl;
Rejoice, Saint George, blessed pilgrim of Christ!

Kontakion 6

You were filled by the mercy of the Comforter, Blessed one; therefore, you gave bread to the hungry, you encouraged the weak at heart, guiding them on the path of faith, and you asked the Lord, through long prayers, to heal the sick, and those whom you had mercy on, sang to God: Alleluia!

Ikos 6

Many of those who saw your life in winter remembered how, entering the bakery, merciful, you melted the ice stuck to your feet. Then, buying a bag of bread, you gave it to the poor who waited for you like a good parent and, thanking you, said:

Rejoice, bridge stretched over the bitterness of life;

Rejoice, harbor of comfort for the helpless;
Rejoice, you who, through prayer, heal the sick;
Rejoice, comforter of those weighed down by burdens and sorrow;
Rejoice, you who gives bread to the hungry;
Rejoice, poor man who gives alms to the poor;
Rejoice, praise of the humbled and broken-hearted;
Rejoice, you who rebuked those always dissatisfied;
Rejoice, traveler on the narrow path of hardship;
Rejoice, you who strengthen the afflicted;
Rejoice, you who shared the received alms with the needy;
Rejoice, merciful and ever-rejoicing Christian;
Rejoice, Saint George, blessed pilgrim of Christ!

Kontakion 7

The Savior of the world, going up the way of the Cross, said to those who followed Him: "weep not for me, but weep for yourselves." Likewise, Saint George, to those who wanted to buy shoes for you, seeing you barefoot in the snow, you answered: "Don't weep for me, for my feet are warmer than yours!" And those who heard your words were amazed, singing to God: Alleluia!

Ikos 7

The Pentecost's tongues of fire, coming down from heaven, enlivened countless people to the love of God. A flame of fire also descended on you, Saint George, so that, making your heart a source of ceaseless prayer and a hearth of the fire of divine love, you ran after Christ on the narrow path. For this, pray that the zeal for salvation may be kindled in us so that we may praise you, saying:

Rejoice, eternal name by calling the name of Jesus;
Rejoice, you who occupied yourself with the work of the mind;
Rejoice, altar into which the great High Priest entered to serve;
Rejoice, for grace warmed your feet and uncovered head;
Rejoice, torch lit by heavenly fire;
Rejoice, confessor full of the power of the Holy Spirit;

Rejoice, hearth in which the uncreated fire burns;
Rejoice, pure heart, in which the Comforter wrote the law of love;
Rejoice, crowned runner for spiritual toil;
Rejoice, you who did not stop before entering through the gates of the Kingdom above;
Rejoice, the one confessed as a saint, since the time of your life;
Rejoice, you who have been called a great hermit and a great apostle;
Rejoice, Saint George, blessed pilgrim of Christ!

Kontakion 8

Savior, the joy you promised to the poor in spirit, shines on the face of Your chosen George the Pilgrim, which is why we praise the heavenly Father, Who willed to hide this gift from the proud and bestow it, through the Spirit Holy, to the humble, and we praise the Most Holy Trinity, One in Essence and Undivided, singing: Alleluia!

Ikos 8

Saint George, the joy that Christ promised to those who follow Him overcame all the sorrows of your life, and you rose above the troubles of the world, for the peace of God was with you. That is why, when you ascended the bright mountain of humility, those who saw your face enveloped in the light of the blessed, marveled and said:

Rejoice, purity that blooms happiness in the world;
Rejoice, you who raise the hymn of peace amid the storm;
Rejoice, voice of Heaven heard in the valley of lamentation;
Rejoice, Psalter with ten strings, singing of Christ;
Rejoice, sweet harp that speaks to the breezes of the Holy Spirit;
Rejoice, loving heart that embraces the whole world in prayer;
Rejoice, pure conscience, tasting the eternal feast;
Rejoice, life of toil, devoted to God with joy;
Rejoice, you who confirmed the glory of the resurrection through the crucifixion of the passions;
Rejoice, hermit who brought the scent of the desert to the city;

Rejoice, you in whom the Kingdom of God has appeared;
Rejoice, torch of virtues placed in the candlestick for the benefit of many;
Rejoice, Saint George, blessed pilgrim of Christ!

Kontakion 9

Through your toils and humility, Saint George, you received from the Holy Spirit the gift of working miracles, in which the sanctity of your life was confirmed, and the distressed, being delivered, learned the saving faith and praised God, singing: Alleluia!

Ikos 9

While teaching the merchants of Târgu Neamt the way of salvation, a Jewish family came to you whose daughter was dying because she could not give birth and you, good man, went to their house and, after marking the tormented one with the sign of the Cross, she immediately gave birth, and, seeing this miracle, they received baptism, saying to you:

Rejoice, intercessor to God for those running to you;
Rejoice, you who show us the way of salvation through wonderful deeds;
Rejoice, you who bring consolation through the sign of the Cross;
Rejoice, you who proved the worth of your life through miracles;
Rejoice, you who confessed Christ through deeds;
Rejoice, you who preached Him also through words;
Rejoice, humble speech, sealed by the grace of the miracle;
Rejoice, you who showed the world the power of the Christian faith;
Rejoice, confession sealed by the Holy Spirit;
Rejoice, holy dough, which leavens the world's lump;
Rejoice, praise, and joy of the people of the new Covenant;
Rejoice, apostolic preacher of the Gospel;
Rejoice, Saint George, blessed pilgrim of Christ!

Kontakion 10

Saint George, in your life, those hostile united: you chose wilderness and solitude, but we see you surrounded by the love of the faithful; you were rough with your body, but you were overjoyed; you despised praise and glory, but God glorified you with the gift of working miracles. And we, convinced by these, sing to the Almighty: Alleluia!

Ikos 10

You were glorified by God when, not being welcomed on the train, you did not grieve, but the train did not start until they reverently brought you back to your place of pilgrimage. For this glorious miracle, we praise you:

Rejoice, man of Heaven, who overcomes the laws of nature;
Rejoice, glorified pilgrim, whom the elements serve;
Rejoice, you who are above material things through Christ;
Rejoice, you who did not resist when you were humiliated;
Rejoice, you who were known to travelers as a pious man;
Rejoice, for they said that the train would not start without you;
Rejoice, for, after you returned, the train immediately started;
Rejoice, for all, seeing the miracle, glorified God;
Rejoice, you who strengthened the preaching with wonderful signs;
Rejoice, humble man, who did not allow thoughts of vain glory;
Rejoice, you in whom the Lord fulfills His promises;
Rejoice, protector of faithful pilgrims and travelers;
Rejoice, Saint George, blessed pilgrim of Christ!

Kontakion 11

Kind ascetic, you have conquered the deception of life, the trickery of the demons, the spirit of the world, and all the illusions born out of sin through prayer, vigil, and fasting. This is why Christ revealed you as a chosen apostle, who amazed even those of other faiths, and seeing the work of the Holy Spirit, we sing: Alleluia!

Ikos 11

When the Son of God revealed the Gospel of Peace to the people, multitudes of sinners, whitening their garments through repentance, appeared as flowers of Heaven in the world. Chosen and well-scented flower, we also see you, Saint George, for which we say to you:

Rejoice, sapling grown from Christ's Vine;
Rejoice, bringer of rich spiritual fruit;
Rejoice, you who had as disciples abbots, priests, and monks;
Rejoice, wonderful counselor, who made many happy;
Rejoice, the one whose life even the Jews marveled at;
Rejoice, for one of them called you revelation;
Rejoice, spiritual man, living in vigils and fasting;
Rejoice, the one revealed by God as a miracle worker;
Rejoice, follower of the Mother of Light;
Rejoice, lily that did not lose its beauty among thorns;
Rejoice, fragrance that gladdens the heavenly inhabitants;
Rejoice, you who now live in the gardens of Heaven;
Rejoice, Saint George, blessed pilgrim of Christ!

Kontakion 12

Like a brave soldier, you fought the good fight; like a watchful watchman, you conquered the night of this life; like a wise maiden, you filled your candle with the oil of love, and when your heart's longing was fulfilled, your pious soul ascended to heaven where you received the unfading crown of glory from the hand of Christ, to Whom you sing: Alleluia!

Ikos 12

When your disciples asked you about the end of your life, you told them: 'I will die when the nations are unsettled and when there will be a celebration at my death, and they will ring the bells in the country.' Thus, your earthly life ended on the glorious feast of the Assumption of the Mother of God when the sound of the bells also brought the news of the Reunification War. So, remembering your prophecy, we sing to you:

Rejoice, you who foreknew the hour of the end;
Rejoice, zealous pilgrim, who has reached the desired One;
Rejoice, you who were taken to the grave by countless crowds;
Rejoice, you who were blessed with many disciples;
Rejoice, traveler not robbed by the thieves of the air;
Rejoice, height to which we look with reverence;
Rejoice, the one buried in the princely court of Voivode Stephen;
Rejoice, you who performed miracles even at the grave;
Rejoice, for when the disciples wanted to carry your relics to Râşca you had not agreed;
Rejoice, for the cart and horses set off towards the Văratec Monastery;
Rejoice, the one glorified by all for this unusual sign!
Rejoice, the one as zealous as Saint Joseph of Văratec!
Rejoice, Saint George, blessed pilgrim of Christ!

Kontakion 13

O elected of Christ, Saint George, you who have well completed the journey of life, pray to the merciful God for us, who are in the desert of the world, to deliver us from the fog of sorrow that comes from sin and to acquire the light of joy that comes from virtues, and by saving us from the delusion of life, let us sing together with you to the Most Holy Trinity: Alleluia!

Ikos 1

Saint George, your heart was pierced from a young age by the call of the Savior, Whom you followed throughout your life; thus, barefooted, with your head uncovered, and carrying the Gospel of love in your hands, you became a sight to angels and men and arrived victorious in the heavenly Canaan, where you pray for those who sing to you:

Rejoice, pure youthfulness dedicated to God;
Rejoice, pinnacle of piety, which your blessed family marveled at;
Rejoice, pilgrim in the footsteps of the Savior in the Holy Land;

Rejoice, supplicant of humble spirit and broken heart;
Rejoice, you who lived all your life barefoot and with your head uncovered;
Rejoice, you who carried the Gospel among people incessantly;
Rejoice, ascetic who lived in the city as in the desert;
Rejoice, willingly poor who brings joy to the poor;
Rejoice, lover of the Psalter, which you learned by heart;
Rejoice, you who lived in prayer, vigil, and fasting;
Rejoice, you who knew the hour of your end, with prophetic eyes;
Rejoice, testimony and praise of public priesthood;
Rejoice, Saint George, blessed pilgrim of Christ!

Kontakion 1

All faithful, come to praise Saint George the Pilgrim who delighted the angels and called people to spiritual life through his wonderful life; for, zealously increasing the ardent gift of seeking and confessing God in travels, churches, and holy toils, he had become a source of joy and intercessor for those singing: Rejoice, Saint George, blessed pilgrim of Christ!

Prayer

Holy and righteous God-pleasing George the Pilgrim, seeing that the day of life is coming to an end and the shadows of the night are settling, the close friends are moving away from us, youth and health are withering every day, great thoughts are dissipating like an illusion, and the Judge is at the doors, engulfed in the darkness of despair, we look for your messages! Saint George, ask God the Merciful to grant us the confession of the thief, the repentance of the publican, and the tears of the sinful woman! Stop, through your prayers, the rivers of passions, dry up the abyss of sins, and guide us to thc harbor of God's will. Dispel the temptations coming from the flesh, devils, and the world, which trouble us with unseemly desires, for you have received the gift of being heard from God. O Saint George, fill our hearts with joy and gratefulness for the gifts received from God, enlighten the darkness of our lives so that looking at your astounding life, we may no longer be ungrateful;

but content with our bread and protection, let us be saved through your intercession, glorifying the Father and the Son and the Holy Spirit, the Trinity, One in Essence and Undivided, now and ever and to the ages of ages. Amen.

Biography

Saint George (Lazar) the Pilgrim was born in the village of Șugag, in Alba county, in 1846, at a time when Transylvania was part of the Habsburg Empire. From a young age he liked fasting and solitude, praying in the village church, and finding remote places to converse with God. He especially loved reading the Psalter.

He married a young woman named Pelagia at the age of 24 and was blessed by God with five children. Even as a husband and a father, he did not abandon his Christian duties of work, prayer, fasting, and almsgiving. Though he himself lived in poverty, he always loved the poor. To all of them he would say: "Do not be disturbed, God cares to feed us; it is our duty to constantly pray and to do His will." Through such words he encouraged himself and others. For this reason he was always at peace, with a bright face and gentle heart. Unceasing prayer and heavenly joy were his companions till the end of his life.

After fourteen years of marriage, with the approval of his wife, George went with several pilgrims to worship at the Tomb of the Lord in 1883 in the Holy Land. He took with him only a Gospel and Psalter. For forty days he visited the Tomb of the Lord three times a day, attending the various services. Then he went to the other places: Bethlehem, Jericho, Jordan, Nazareth, Tabor. At the Cave of Saint Xenophon he met a hermit who prophesied to him that he would not be a monk, but would live from place to place, in poverty and unceasing prayer; only so would he save his soul and kindle godliness in the hearts of many people.

After this, he remained in the desert of upper Egypt for forty days in strict fasting, facing many temptations from the devil. Sometimes the enemy frightened him with beasts and poisonous snakes, other times he struggled with hunger, thirst, heat and mosquitoes. Once, the devil threw off his hat from his head, wishing to anger him, but the mighty soldier promised God that he would go until death with his head uncovered. Then the devil threw his boots away; for this reason all his life he was barefoot both in summer and winter. Once the devil appeared to him in the form of a plowman, who praised him for his endeavor, to make him fall into the temptation of pride, but the wise George conquered him with humble thoughts. Thus, with the help of God and with great perseverance, he passed the test of forty days of fasting, escaping from all the temptations that came either from the infirmities of the flesh or from the devil. Soon after this, the good man went to Jerusalem, where he worshiped at the Tomb of the Lord. As he entered the church to light the candle at the Holy Sepulcher, as an unequivocal and comforting proof that his prayers and fasting were received by God, the candle in his hand lit by itself.

Then, after a year and a half on Mount Athos, he returned to his country, having been away for three years. Back home he continued to be harassed by the devil to frighten him away from his God-pleasing struggles. After living with his family for a few years, and having put his children's affairs in order, he retired as a pilgrim to the monasteries of Moldavia in 1890. He went from church to church where he prayed almost all night; he walked hurriedly, barefoot and head uncovered. Nearly every year he made a pilgrimage to Jerusalem, guiding several other pilgrims.

George established himself permanently in the city of Piatra Neamţ in 1895, living in asceticism like a true hermit in the bell tower of the Church of Saint John the Baptist, built by Stephen the Great, in the middle of the city for 26 years, until his death. There he labored alone in fasting and prayer, summer and winter, without fire, without bed, without a coat, and without shoes on his feet, living in God's grace. In a short time he became known to priests, monks, and laity who valued him as a true spiritual man.

He slept no more than three hours a night, made hundreds of prostrations, walked the streets during the day barefoot with head uncovered whispering the psalms. He did not return to his cell until he completed the entire Psalter. Monday, Wednesday and Friday he did not eat anything until the next day, and if it was a Great Feast, he tasted something in the evening. The other days he would eat once a day. He spoke to men only about God and the spiritual life, and when he did not speak with his tongue and lips, he preached through his complete silence, always carrying in his arms either the Gospel or the Psalter.

He often went into a bakery and bought a bag of bread that someone would take to the tower. At the time of his return, a lot of poor people gathered around him, and the happy George shared his loaves. Those who demanded money he gave them what he had received on the way. The wise man conversed with each one, encouraging them, counseling them and praying for them, and men felt the grace and the mercy of God descend upon them through the prayers and counsel of the Holy One.

All the surrounding monasteries he exceedingly loved, but especially Bistrita, where the icon of Saint Anna was. Near the Sihastria Monastery, George dug up a hole in his hiding place, praying there almost all day; and when he returned to the monastery, he was thankful to Father John, the abbot of this monastery: "Today I was in heaven!"

Once, the Saint wanted to take the train somewhere, but he boarded without a ticket, because he had no money. The conductor, who by no means knew him, took him off the train at the first station, though travelers who knew him asked him to let him go where he wished. George went off and walked along the railroad, bidding farewell and offering his blessing. When the conductor then tried to start the train, it would not start. They then changed locomotives, but still it would not start. Then one of the station officials said to go get George, because he was a holy man, and on his account the Lord would not allow the train to start. They ran after him, brought him up, got him in the train and immediately the train started and left the station.

Another miracle, narrated by Father Cleopa Ilie, took place in Târgu Neamţ. A young Jewish woman could not bear her child and was ready to die. Many doctors came, but nothing happened. Then her relatives went to George, and they asked him to pray for her. When George opened the door of her house, he cried, "Open up with God and the Mother of God!" And immediately her womb opened and she gave birth, and the Holy One went and crossed the child's head. She became healthy, and she and her baby were baptized, and named him George after the Saint. And then all her relatives in Târgu Neamţ were baptized.

The day of his death he had known beforehand, and he uttered these prophetic words: "I will die when the people are troubled, and at my death they will celebrate, and they will ring the bells in the land." He reposed on August 15, 1916 and was buried in the town cemetery. His funeral was just as he predicted, with countless people in attendance. Eighteen years later, in the summer of 1934, one of his disciples, wishing to move his relics to Râşca, came with the train to Piatra Neamţ, and he set off on his way. But by divine order, the train did not reach Râşca, but to the Văratec Monastery, in which the tomb can still be venerated until today. He is known as "Grandpa George" among the pious faithful. His relics, kept beneath the main church in the monastery, are fragrant. He was glorified by the Romanian Orthodox Church in 2017.

Books published by Nun Christina Oceanitissa:

The collective works of St Nektarios of Aegina.
The Philokalia 5: The full text in English.
The collective works of Elder Cleopa.
The Anacreontic Poems by Saint Sophronius Patriarch of Jerusalem.
The Life of Saint Paul of Thebes the First Hermit.
The Devil: The Cause of Sin by Saint John of Kronstadt.
Faith and the Orthodox Church by Saint John of Kronstadt.
The Monastic Rule of Saint Pachomius the Great.
Supplicatory Canon and Akathist to St Paisios.
Supplicatory Canon and Akathist to St Porphyrios.
Supplicatory Canon and Akathist to St George.
Supplicatory Canon and Akathist to St Anastasia.
Supplicatory Canon and Akathist to St Anna.
Supplicatory Canon and Akathist to St John the Russian.
Supplicatory Canon and Akathist to St Ephraim of Nea Makri.
Supplicatory Canon and Akathist to St John Maximovitch.
Supplicatory Canon and Akathist to St Dimitri.
Supplicatory Canon and Akathist to St Joseph the Hesycast.
Supplicatory Canon and Akathist to St Luke the Surgeon.
Supplicatory Canon and Akathist to St John the Baptist.
The Way of a Pilgrim.
Conversation with a Grieving Man by St Dimitri of Rostov.
The Inner Man by St Dimitri of Rostov.
Orthodox Prayer Book.
Daily Orthodox Prayer book.

www.ingramcontent.com/pod-product-compliance
Lightning Source LLC
LaVergne TN
LVHW010512160826
845677LV00012B/2813

* 9 7 9 8 8 4 8 9 2 1 9 8 4 *